You

Disgust

Me

You Disgust Me

L. De Voss

ISBN: 978-1-63441-013-7

DEDICATION

This collection is dedicated to anyone who is between the ages of seventeen and twenty-two, because that's how old I was when I wrote them. It's a bitch, ain't it?

Published
by
Toad & Fox

CONTENTS

You Disgust Me   1

Perceptions of You - I   2

Perceptions of You - II   3

Perceptions of You - III   4

Perceptions of You - IV   5

Four Steps She Took   6

Rage   8

I Thank You and Goodbye   10

Better Off Without   11

An Ending   12

West Indies   13

Looking Down   14

My Heart   15

Such a Pity   16

I Can't Explain   17

Loverboy Get Lost   18

Mother My Mother   19

Blurred Vision   20

Ciao   21

A New Dance   22

Who Is?   23

The Big Question   24

Words   25

A Cycle of Subtraction   26

Working   28

Poor Creatures and Complaints   29

Old News   30

Revenge   31

The Quiet Ones   32

Torture   33

Ancient History   34

The Truth   35

A Play   36

The Rockies   37

Remember   38

You Disgust Me

you
disgust me
touching and then turning
listening and not learning
slowly
cutting
deep
forever trying to excuse yourself
forever finding the reasons which master your thought
you
disgust me
reaching out and only taking
using me for your own making
playing
games
for keeps

Perceptions of You - I

and I do cry
I spend my time in agony working for you
using my time
using my life
I move slowly
for fear of breaking the bond too quickly
afraid that you'll go away too fast
recede as the tide is secretly pulled by the moon
I don't even have you
and I dwell on the pain of losing you
and I do cry
for hours
for days
deep silent crying
I question everything
I question nothing
and I can still hear the ringing of your answers

Perceptions of You - II

Move!
he said
Out of the way!
Can't you see you're a distraction?
Can't you see?

Oh, never mind!
he said
you'll never understand
you'll never be a man with things to see
important thoughts to finish

You're a distraction!
he said
a luminous point in time serving no function
no logic
no movement

Move! he said

Perceptions of You - III

walking in the sun
I see spots
I see small spheres that glow and float in the breeze
sometimes I try to catch them

they burn my fingers

it's not a painful burn
it's more like a warning burn
a
don't-touch-me-I'm-only-here-to-be-appreciated
burn

Perceptions of You - IV

when I work my hands slowly over your body
I think about contour and contouring
my fingers glide easily
my hands feel smooth
I touch you where you are contoured most
and I draw away in fear and mistrust
I don't understand your body
I sit in awe sometimes
at the difference between you and me

sit and talk
we say
touch and go
we play

cautiously
pulling into our heads
I sometimes wonder what it really should be like
in bed
or on the floor
or wherever we happen to fall

as though we're out to prove ourselves
to some invisible standard
that lays with us throughout the night

Four Steps She Took

O' drear the night she doomed herself
O' hard the heart that cared

I worked so quietly
I moved so calmly
I scared myself
into thinking the time had come

Please! I cried
Is it time?
Is it time to come out?
my shell is so tight and it shrinks daily in its feel
no room to breathe, oh please
I want out!

O' drear the night she doomed herself
O' hard the heart that cared

I'm tired of self-deception
I'm weary of hatred
the scorn
you speak so pretty and wise
maneuvers and mannerisms in disguise
you use me
trick me
take me and torment me with guile
I loathe the space in which you sleep
and deep the piercing blows I'd send
if only you would smile

O' drear the night she doomed herself
O' hard the heart that cared

see me dancing?
see my grace?

that one so foolish could calm my face
is surely a feat to have
try
no don't
please do and wait
I'll change
I'll grow
I'll hide my very thought
I wouldn't want to conflict
pray no
for then I would be different

O' drear the night she doomed herself
O' hard the heart that cared

in darkness now I sit
and dwell upon my fright
so quietly
as if the dead could speak
I listen as you laugh

Rage

angry at the traps you lay for me I'm angry
Come in!
Let me warm you with the fire of my heart!
you say

and a false heart you lead me to
with your gentle urgings
your peaceful ways
I sit and shiver for there is no fire
only a small piece of coal
which I rub between my hands
and smooth upon my body
I return black with despair
to my own womb
and my own meager warmth

Share!
you cry
Share and your blaze will expand
within you!
Take from me for I have to give!
you say again and again
Try to be open!
Reach out!

I get spit in return
you mock me behind my back
with my thoughts of depression
that spill out when we call each other friends
and twist my words to torture me

yes, I'm angry
hateful with your push-me pull-me attitude
your stand-alone-and-I'll-save-you façade
go ahead
ask me again why I fantasize killing you

I Thank You and Goodbye

I thank you
for so cleverly disposing of me
when you thought me inconvenient
I appreciate
the swiftness of your release
and the making of me into a nonentity
when I belonged

Does it not matter that you reduced me to tears
on that street?
Does it mean so little to you
the crime you dealt so well?
The verbal blade that cut so deep?

I hate you for what you did to me
I shall never forgive the game you played
Are we not beyond such games?
Are we not past that point of sloppy revenge?

go ahead then
reverse and dally
I have to go now

Better Off Without

so this is the problem, you see
too many one-liners
too many open sentences
too many words without definition

so this is the problem, you see
too little caring
too little respect
too little honesty

you come into my life
odd hours
strange habits
destruction

you bother me
you make me laugh
you criticize me
you praise me
you make me laugh
you touch me
tease me
torment me
you make me laugh

so this is the solution, you see
to stop worrying
to stop analyzing
to stop laughing

An Ending

I said goodbye and you said goodbye
I heard the words over the phone
as if I wasn't there at all
as if sitting outside myself
watching and waiting for the sound to fall
I was not there

oh yes, it hurt
for a long time it hurt
a small death occurred and you're the one who died

I said goodbye and you said goodbye
I didn't mean to be so foolish about it
dragging it out
leading you on
or, so I thought I did
but didn't you drag and lead just as much as me?
didn't you write this play when you said
I don't think that I can ever touch you again . . .

I said goodbye and you said goodbye
we both said goodbye
now you aren't there
I don't yet know what that's like
it's been quite a while since I've been alone

I'm going to miss you
please miss me too

L. De Voss

West Indies

it's quiet here and the day moves slowly
the people are poor
they wander their time away
you say hello
you don't
the rooster knows I'm watching
and crows accordingly

I met a young man on the beach today
exercising
I asked if I could learn his movements
Where did you get them?

The men in prison, he replies
they taught them to me

he waits for my surprise
my fear
my whatever

I smile
from dangerous men can be discovered useful things
I am unaware of implications

Looking Down

I like touching my breasts
they're round
and soft
and pressable
I feel their weight in my hands
milk sacks for the completion of a cycle
it's a good weight
a demanding weight
it cries to be comforted
supported
so I wrap them up
and carry them with me wherever I go
at the beach I warm them in the sun
cool them in the water
it's a pleasant feeling
one that can't be shared
only exposed

L. De Voss

My Heart

preserve my heart for me
and keep it in a wooden case
carry my soul with you
wrapped up in silken lace

these two things
are to me most dear
and in time to come
it will be most clear

my heart is tempered
with silent sigh
my soul is unified
in quiet cry

I study you
as you study me
making our minds up
on eternity

Such a Pity

it hurts and it hurts
but I plow right through
push it aside with both arms
and lean forward forever forward
tripping on my lips
drooling on my toes Oops! pardon me
I didn't see you standing in my way
as a matter of fact I wasn't even looking
such a pity
what a shame
and it still hurts

I Can't Explain

I'm selfish
intellectually I want to give
emotionally I can't see straight
I want to release
but I fear you'll walk away
or grow angry
or laugh
yes even laugh
I do it myself
I don't know what I'm talking about anymore
I can't think straight
I ramble and ramble
hoping to reach some climax
hoping that somewhere in my drivel
I'll reach out and grasp some
deep
dark
secret
an Ugly Truth that will save my life
save me
ha
you see I do laugh
I don't know who I'm saying it to anymore
I'm tired
I'm so tired
I don't want to understand
I can't explain anymore

Loverboy Get Lost

yes your touch is sweet
and your hands are gentle
but let me again repeat
just where is the mental?

your smile is divine
I think your laugh is great
all of this is fine
but hardly makes a mate

each day in life I want to train
be useful and worthwhile
I want to seed within my brain
beliefs that make me smile

my values run upon this wire
don't slip; it is quite thin
since this is all I do require
your chances are most slim

I guess I'll say goodbye to you
and think about you well
how good you'll be in a year or two
well, only time will tell

Mother My Mother

mother my mother
it's to you that I write
to explain you my absence
to explain you my fright

it's hard to say when the words first began
I found them entertaining
they told me stories and made me laugh
then they grew bolder and questioned me
it became terrifying when they commanded me
and now
well, now they just answer me

mother oh my mother
it's to you that I write
by the cool of this fountain
by the cool of this night

a love story I saw
it hurts to think of love
it tears me to touch a man now
I grieve for my body and the delights that I deny it
happily they clasped in this story I saw
yet their expressions painted painful
menace in their smiles

mother be my mother
it's to you that I write
hold my mind's confusion
keep my wisdom's sight

please

Blurred Vision

we are to them what they are to us
and if one could stand on the between
and face both ways at once
the view would be the same
both coming and going
both giving and taking
alive and dead
the same
we are all the same
no difference
no depth

Ciao

Loose as in noose
I'll hang myself on Monday

Red as in dead
I'll sleep the better Tuesday

Long as in gone
I'll leave the world on Wednesday

Reach as in preach
My friends will hear on Thursday

Me as in see
The gates will open Friday

How as in now
The hand will fall on Sat'day

Task as in flask
To drink my peace on Sunday

A New Dance

I want to kill myself
it's a common thought
enters my head almost every day
it's hard to talk about it to most people
they get nervous
they twitch
Oh please don't kill yourself, they whimper
Please don't commit suicide

I know why they say it
it would make them look bad
not me
no, I would sink into oblivion
but they would have to keep looking at each other
feeling sorry for each other
Why feel sorry when you can do yourself in?

it's so much simpler, of course, to go on living
everyone expects it until you drop dead
never thinking to lie down and die
never thinking
I truly do want to kill myself
but I'm not quite sure
whether or not it would be more interesting to live
that stops me for now

also, if you do do The Do-Yourself-In
you do yourself in
and no one much cares one way or the other
they go on
because they want to
think they have to
besides, we get in each other's way

L. De Voss

Who Is?

catch me when I'm low
and raise me when I'm down
but don't let me sit there
please
press me forward
no explanations are needed
no excuses required
I give you permission
it's too easy to turn away
it's too simple to pretend and so unnecessary
I'm the diameter
you're the circumference
without me you wouldn't exist
without you I serve no function
Who is more important?

The Big Question

and a great sadness fell upon her
as she watched her life of lives go by
What is the purpose of all this? she cried
Must everything have a purpose?
came her reply
it wasn't an answer which gave recourse

A misery a misery, she moaned
Shall I spend my time making things for no purpose?
Am I to live only to die
with no understanding of what has passed?

or is it still present
perhaps there is no past and future
maybe we've been fooling ourselves
and there's only the present
to torment and tease us

Words

I HATE WORDS!
those slimy little creatures
who slip
and slide inside my brain
as though it were an amusement park

THEY DRIVE ME NUTS!
always connecting themselves into chains
all too recognizable
all too destructive
spoiling good moods
and
only occasionally content with just confusing me

I CAN'T STAND THEM!
so hideous in their disguise of communication
that they scare almost anyone
into mute anxiety
I mean
Do you really understand me now?

A Cycle of Subtraction

take it away
take it away
let it leave my side
as I worry to my health
and I worry to my pride

for things that claw and cling to me
can creep into my brain
and there the grain they seed in me
forever leaves me lame

so take it away
take it away
let it leave my side
as I worry to my business
and I struggle with the lies

untruth slides silently
and swift through objects bare
the mass produced
unfocused truth
in which there is no care
each artifact lacks sentiment
lies stagnant in its state
an open door
for death to pour
its shadowed lines of hate

oh take it away
please take it away
and let it leave my side
it burns my hands in touching
to cool it I have tried

and yet no ointment will it soothe
the pain it lingers long
it grips and twists my every move
with it I can't go on

yes take it away
oh take it away
and let it leave my side
for if it stays within my life
I know how I will die

a slow and subtle death will spread
through trunk and gentle limb
to eat my heart
in minute parts
useless I will have been

Working

my first day for a full-time job
I look at the clock
and wonder what time I should leave
I wonder if I'll ever leave

time plays tricks on me
calling to me that it won't take long
that I'll have enough but not too much

I worry about being early or late
appearing eager or in haste
Should I smile my first day?
Or hold a false fear in disguise for respect?
Should I outdo myself?
or lay back
insisting that there is greater challenge
greater challenge by whose standards, I might add

my first day and already I'm planning my life

Poor Creatures and Complaints

Men say:
a man is a bum who cannot support his wife
Women say:
a woman is inadequate when she has no career of her
own

Men say:
a woman who does not allow her husband sexual
freedom is insensitive to his needs
Women say:
a man who plays around too often is a lout and not to
be trusted

Men say:
a woman should play all the roles in bed that her
husband wants
Women say:
a man should not do with his wife what he does with
a whore

Men say:
a man should never be questioned
Women say:
a woman should trust in herself

Men say:
a man cannot be understood by a woman
Women say:
no one understands anyone

the men confuse
the women excuse
Haven't we got something better to do?

Old News

you are virtuous
I am cold
you have wisdom
I am old
you are dashing
I'm a slut
you are adventure
I'm a rut
you are useful
I'm a toy
you're not a girl
and I'm not a boy

Revenge

you were the small child
whose mother punished
by putting a favorite toy high upon the shelf
out of reach

now
you knew that eventually you would have it back
but instead of accepting that it was only a toy
it became more than a toy
it became a need
a desire
an obsession
you want it back
you got angry
you swore revenge upon your mother
and her power over you
What right has she to take from you?

you had a tantrum
screaming for the toy
but screaming for so much more
your mother didn't listen
she destroyed the toy
Didn't you want the toy?

to this day
you still believe that revenge is a tactic
and not a need
a desire
an obsession
you don't want the toy
you just want to win

The Quiet Ones

we are the quiet ones
despite the boisterous loudness
the anguished screams
we are truly the quiet ones
for we accept the decisions of men
with such patience
with such faith
that the true life we could share goes
deep within us
so let us laugh
let us dance
let us show the world there is no pain
yes we are the quiet ones
and time will pass again

Torture

I resist
you come on
I resist
you come on
I resist
you go away
I succumb
you aren't there

Ancient History

some say history repeats itself
retraces its footprints upon the same sand
it's not the repetition that annoys me
it's the variations it makes
the turmoil it causes
I have grown accustomed to my surroundings
I wish no surprises in my life
no meaningless actions
no wastrel wants
so I remain upon my bridge
I add one plank each day
god knows what I'll span
I've been doing it for so long
I can't see which side I started from

The Truth

meaningless actions I take

and I sit and I wait
and I sit and I wait

motionless movements I make

and I sit and I wait
and I sit and I wait

I hate myself when I don't create
I deny my sense of birth

I hate myself when I congregate
I deny my sense of truth

it's either meaningless actions
or actionless meanings

I just want to win

A Play

so you are alright
and I am alright

you are here
and I am there
together we'll form a play

it all began over there
yessir right here

over there you
I enjoy being here

I prefer to be there
I'm thinking of you here

I miss you there
you are right here

there is no reason or excuse for this
on the other hand
here is a perfect defense

therefore

L. De Voss

The Rockies

the mountains call for discovery
the mountains ache for your touch
they rise and tumble
in a brooding plan
they breathe the clouds in a rush

the mountains are a place of learning
exploration is their name
expeditions do not defile
their long and lonesome smile
it's the land which none may claim

the mountains are your home
somber where they stay
seek out your information
go round the world once more
for they will wait quite patiently
until you find your way

Remember

cry aloud for all the sorrow
sing the song of the oppressed
but remember all the laughs
the funny things that passed
and see me as I am
please
just as I am

ABOUT THE AUTHOR

Nothing to see here. Just move along.

I have.

- L